A Smart Kid's Guide to

Social Networking Online

David J. Jakubiak

PowerKiDS
press
New York

Published in 2010 by The Rosen Publishing Group, Inc.
29 East 21st Street, New York, NY 10010

First Edition

Editor: Amelie von Zumbusch
Book Design: Julio Gil
Photo Researcher: Jessica Gerweck

Photo Credits: Cover © www.iStockphoto.com/Margot Petrowski; p. 5 © M. Thomsen/zefa/Corbis; p. 6 Jose Luis Pelaez/Getty Images; p. 9 Ryan McVay/Getty Images; p. 10 Garry Wade/Getty Images; p. 13 Bruce Laurance/Getty Images; p. 14 Nossa Productions/Getty Images; p. 17 B2M Productions/Getty Images; p. 18 © LWA-Dann Tardif/Corbis; p. 21 © Jim Cummins/Corbis.

Library of Congress Cataloging-in-Publication Data

Jakubiak, David J.
    A smart kid's guide to social networking online / David J. Jakubiak. — 1st ed.
        p. cm. — (Kids online)
    Includes index.
    ISBN 978-1-4042-8119-6 (library binding) — ISBN 978-1-4358-3358-6 (pbk.) — ISBN 978-1-4358-3359-3 (6-pack)
    1. Online social networks—Juvenile literature. 2. Internet and children—Juvenile literature. 3. Internet—Safety measures. 4. Safety education—Juvenile literature. I. Title.
    HM742.J35 2010
    302.23'1—dc22
                                    2009006377

Manufactured in the United States of America

Contents

A Web of Networks

Have you ever heard of online social networks? These online communities are places where people can have fun and get in touch with friends. Even if you have not heard the term "social networks," you may have spent time on one of these sites. For example, Millsberry, Club Penguin, and Tweegee are all online social networks. They let you chat with people around the world. People use social-networking sites to start **blogs** and play games. People trade messages about movies, TV shows, and sports on these sites, too.

If you use them safely, online social networks can be lots of fun. They let you use your imagination and offer a place to say what you think.

Online social networks are on the Internet, so you can visit these communities at any time and from any place. All you need is a computer with an Internet connection.

If you are thinking about joining an online social network, consider asking a friend who is already a member to show you the games and other things you can do on the network.

More than Games

There are lots of things you can do on an online social network. Many kids use online social networks to play games. Sites such as www.tweegee.com and www.webkinz.com offer games of all kinds. Some games even help teach reading and math. Many of the games on social-networking sites are played alone. Others, called multiplayer games, are played by big groups of people.

However, networking sites have more than games. Many social networks also let kids set up their own Web sites, where they can write stories and send messages. These sites are a great way to get used to using a computer. They also teach kids **responsibility** and problem solving.

Looking at a Network

Going to an online social-networking site is like visiting a new town. When you visit a networking site, look around to see what is there. Try some of the games. If you can, watch how the people who are using the site talk to each other. Ask yourself, "How might I use this site?"

Online social networks are set up like communities. One example is www.millsberry.com. On this site, users make and control a "buddy" that lives in an online town called Millsberry. The buddy can go to school, shop, and play in Millsberry. You may see **cereal** boxes on the site. This is because it is run by a company that makes cereal.

It can be lots of fun to check out an online social network with your friends. If you all like the site, you can decide to meet up on the site again later.

A teenage brother, sister, or cousin can likely teach you
about social networking. You may need to find your own network, though.
Teenagers often belong to networks that do not allow kids.

Is It for You?

There are many online social networks. Some are free, while others cost money. Some are for kids in elementary and middle school. Other networks, such as MySpace and Facebook, are for high-school kids and adults. Most networking sites have **age limits**. Always respect these age limits. Never try to pretend to be older than you really are online. Age limits are there to keep kids safe.

Have an adult make sure you are old enough to use a social-networking site before you sign up to become a member of the site. For example, you must be at least 6 years old to join WebKinz. Tweegee is for kids who are between the ages of 8 and 18.

Know the Rules

Always check out a social-networking site with an adult before you join it. Have the adult read and explain the site's rules, or terms of use, so that you know what is allowed. Find out where to get help on the site, in case you ever forget your **password** or have other problems.

To join most online social networks, you will have to give an e-mail address where the site can send you messages. For example, the site may send a message to start your **membership**. Many networking sites will also ask you to pick a password and **user name**. Do not use your real name as your user name. Everyone on a site can see user names.

Ask a trusted adult to look on while you fill out the online forms needed to join a social-networking site. The adult can answer any questions you have about what to put on the form.

When you are filling out your profile for a
social-networking site, you can ask a friend, brother, or sister to help you figure
out what sorts of facts you want to list.

Your Online You

Many online social networks let you set up a profile. This is a page where you tell people about yourself. Do not put too many facts on your profile. Never put a picture of yourself online. Instead, pick a picture of an object or an **icon** for your profile. Do not enter facts about yourself, such as your age, phone number, home address, or school. When you are done setting it up, make sure that only the people you pick can see your profile.

Most sites let you set limits on whom you can chat with and what you can do. For example, some sites let you chat by either typing your own words or by picking from a list of common sayings.

Bullies in Your Network

Even if you follow all of a networking site's rules, you may have to deal with an online bully. Bullies are people who say bad things about other people and try to scare them. Online bullies often write messages making fun of other people. Bullies may spread around mean and untrue stories about other kids, too. If a bully bothers you, or you see a bully picking on someone else, do not get into a fight. Instead, send a message to the site explaining what you saw. It is also a good idea to talk to a trusted adult any time that a bully bothers you.

If you have not yet had trouble with bullies, plan ahead. Learn how to report bullies. Then you will know what to do if trouble starts!

Getting messages from an online bully can make you feel hurt and alone. However, there are many people you can turn to for help when a bully bothers you.

If you received messages from an online predator, remember that it was not your fault. Predators often make kids feel like they are to blame. However, the predators are the ones who did something wrong.

Beware of Predators

While having fun online, keep an eye out for online predators. Online predators are people who try to fool kids into thinking they are their friends. Predators ask kids to do **inappropriate** things.

You will be less likely to run into online predators if you chat online only with people you know in real life. If someone whom you met online asks you your age or where you live, do not respond. Never agree to meet someone whom you have met online in person. If you think that a predator is trying to reach you, tell a trusted adult. A parent, teacher, or guardian would be a good person to talk to. This adult may need to get in touch with the police.

Leaving a Network

The time may come when you want to leave a social network. If so, you will need to erase your profile. Each site has its own rules for ending memberships. Some sites ask people who want their profiles erased to fill out a form. Other sites end the memberships of anyone who has not used the site for 90 days. Check your e-mail after asking to end a membership. You may need to take more steps to finish the job.

If you leave one networking site, you may want to join another. Discovering online social networks can be lots of fun. Stay safe, be careful, and enjoy what they have to offer.

Spending time on an online social network can be lots of fun. If you get tired of one network, though, you can always leave it and sign up for another one.

Safety Tips

- Personal facts do not belong in profiles or blogs. Keep them off the Internet.

- Keep your time online to 2 hours or fewer each day.

- Have an adult use **security software** to block out bad words and sites that are not meant for kids.

- Keep your passwords to yourself. If someone finds out a password, change it.

- If someone puts your personal facts online, have an adult contact the site right away to get them taken down.

- Spend some time checking out a site before you sign up. Make sure it is right for you.

- Always have a parent or guardian read over the site's rules with you when you sign up for a social-networking site.

Glossary

age limits (AYJ LIH-mets) Rules that say how old a person must be to do something.

blogs (BLOGZ) Web sites where people share thoughts or facts.

cereal (SIR-ee-ul) Food made from grain.

icon (EYE-kon) A picture that stands for something on a computer.

inappropriate (in-nuh-PROH-pree-ut) Not suitable or right.

membership (MEM-bur-ship) Being a member of something.

password (PAS-wurd) A secret combination of letters or numbers that lets someone enter something.

responsibility (rih-spon-sih-BIH-lih-tee) Something that a person must take care of or complete.

security software (sih-KYUR-ih-tee SAWFT-wer) A tool that keeps a computer or the person using it safe.

user name (YOO-zer NAYM) The name a person uses on a computer.

Index

Web Sites

Due to the changing nature of Internet links, PowerKids Press has developed an online list of Web sites related to the subject of this book. This site is updated regularly. Please use this link to access the list: www.powerkidslinks.com/onlin/network/